JOURNEY OF LOVE

God Moving In our Hearts and Lives

Maureen Conroy, RSM, D.Min.

The Upper Room Spiritual Center
P.O. BOX 1104
W. BANGS AVENUE & ROUTE No. 33
NEPTUNE, NEW JERSEY 07753
Telephone: (732) 922-0550

The Upper Room Spiritual Center

P.O. BOX 1104
W. BANGS AVENUE & ROUTE No. 33
NEPTUNE, NEW JERSEY 07753
Telephone: (732) 922-0550

Library of Congress Cataloging-in-Publication Data

Conroy, Maureen, 1948 -
    Journey of Love: God moving in our hearts and lives/
    Maureen Conroy

    p. cm.
    ISBN 0-8091-3413-6 (pbk.)
    1. Spiritual life - Catholic Church.
    2. Catholic Church - Doctrines. I. Title.
    BX2350.2C6136   1993
    248.4'82-dc20   93-979
                                                              CIP

Published by Paulist Press, from 1993 - 1998
997 Macarthur Boulevard
Mahwah, New Jersey 07430

Printed and bound in the United States of America by:
Boro Printing, Inc.
200 Broadway
Long Branch, New Jersey 07740
(732) 229-1899

Contents

DEDICATION

I dedicate this book to my friend

Judy Chevalier

who has been a special gift to me
on my spiritual journey.

Introduction

Our Spiritual Journey

Our life is a journey with peaks and valleys, joys and sorrows, births and deaths. Our life in God is a spiritual journey with a variety of movements—darkness and light, slavery and freedom, desolation and consolation, pain and joy, weakness and strength. When we are alive in God, on a journey with God, there appears never to be a dull moment. When our hearts seem to be centered in God, all of a sudden God will bring an area of inner darkness to our awareness, and again there seems to be upheaval. When our relationship with God seems to be trusting and strong, something happens that causes our faith to waver and our trust to be tested. When we think we have expressed all of our feelings to God about a situation, a surge of anger unexpectedly arises within us and throws off our equilibrium.

"Why can't our spiritual journey be steady, predictable, and consistent," we wonder. "God is supposed to be our rock and foundation, yet we seem never to be on solid ground," we groan. We get exasperated with the surprising ways of God and the different ways that we respond.

In this book I reflect on various movements of our hearts and lives that occur as we journey in love with God. I use scriptural passages as the basis for my reflections. Each reflection ends with an invitation for you to be with God in a contemplative way. Through suggesting ways for you to ponder, share with God, listen to God, and respond in concrete ways, I provide an arena for you to be even more personally attentive to and absorbed in God. In the conclusion, I suggest more scriptural prayers and quotes that you can ponder and contemplate. I encourage you to "pray with" these reflections rather than "read through" them. That is, contemplate each one with your heart, imagination, and spiritual senses as well as your mind.

We are all on a journey of love. Our spiritual journey is about letting God make a home in our hearts and surrendering to God's desire to give us fullness of life. It means allowing God to love us unconditionally and to incarnate that love through our loving attitudes and actions. I invite you to pray with these reflections as a way to deepen your intimacy with God and enrich your journey of love.

God Birthing Us

Five Expressions of Love

Now says the Lord, who created you and formed you:
Fear not, for I have redeemed you;
I have called you by name; you are mine.
You are precious in my eyes and glorious, and I love
you. (Isaiah 43:1,4)

God speaks to us very personally through this brief passage. Five specific expressions of God's life-giving love for us are highlighted: creating, redeeming, naming, belonging, and delighting. In these experiences God reveals a fullness of love that is eager to be born in humanity. God communicates a personal love that desires an intimate relationship with each of us.

CREATING

God creates us. In the creative process we see a God who is overflowing with love. "God is a great underground river that no one can dam up and no one can stop," says Meister Eckhart. The very nature of God is to give, so God creates a beautiful world. God's bountiful love cannot be contained. God's creative love cannot be stifled.

God forms us. God takes a deep breath and breathes human life into existence. We are the breath of God. We are the most precious of all of God's creation. God breathed life into us, a life reflecting the God-life. We are made into God's image and likeness. As we look at our image in that great underground river who is God, we see reflected there the Person of God in our person. We are the imprint of God. We are full of God because we are made in the very likeness of God.

We come from the womb of God. Our Mother God has given birth to each of us uniquely. Our Mother God has surrounded us with warmth and tenderness, holding us close to the divine heart. Our Mother God not only brings us to life but also nurtures the divine life within us. Our God is a creative, nurturing, and nourishing Mother of us all.

REDEEMING

The God–life within us, the great underground river, becomes polluted. The clear sparkling water of God's loving presence is tinged with the poison of our self-centeredness and self-seeking. We lose sight of the fresh water of God. The fresh air of God which we breathe is filled with black soot. We are overwhelmed with the pollution of sin and darkness.

"Fear not, for I have redeemed you." Our loving God will not allow us to be lost for long. Our Mother God comes after us: "How could I give you up, or deliver you up.... My heart is overwhelmed, my pity is stirred" (Hosea 11:8). Our Mother God draws us close to the divine heart, pulsating with unconditional love. Our saving God purifies the polluted water and air with redeeming love. We are constantly being reborn and made new.

NAMING

"I have called you by name." God has left an indelible mark within us. Each of us is uniquely the imprint of God, a word of God from all eternity. God not only loves all of us and all of creation, but also loves each of us in a very personal way. God reveals this personal love for each of us by giving us a name. We each have a name of grace. This name is written in God's heart, never to be erased.

Our name gives each of us a unique identity in God. We are God's word spoken, never to be duplicated. The word of God spoken in each of us is represented in our name. God calls us by our name from all eternity. God invites us to listen to this personal call, God's voice speaking our name each day.

BELONGING

"You are mine." We belong to God. This belonging is rooted in a profound intimacy with God. This intimacy is grounded in God's passionate love. God does not love in a distant or stoical way, but in a deeply involved and personal way. The very essence of passionate love is the desire for union. God desires that our hearts be united to God's heart in full communion.

We belong to God more deeply than we belong to ourselves or anyone else; however, our belonging to God does not wipe out our identity. It is in our unique personalities that we are intimate with God. The more we develop our own uniqueness, the more we have to bring to our intimate relationship with God. God desires that the fullness of our humanity be united to the fullness of God's divinity. We are most at home with God when we are at home with ourselves.

DELIGHTING

"You are precious in my eyes." God looks at us with delight. God sees each of us as special. In God's eyes we are precious and beautiful, a masterpiece. "You are glorious, and I love you." God saw all that was created, and saw that it was good. The clear pure water of God's creative love overflows from a heart that delights. God finds joy in each of us. As the prophet Zephaniah says: "God rejoices over you with gladness, and renews you in love; God sings joyfully because of you, as one sings at festivals" (3:17). God is glorified in and through us. "God's greatest glory is a person fully alive," says St. Irenaeus.

CONCLUSION

We see in this brief passage from Isaiah five rich expressions of God birthing us: creating, redeeming, naming, belonging, and delighting. There are so many different ways that God says, "I love you." Let us bask in the sunlight of God's warm and tender love, breathe in the air of God's life-giving and pervasive love, and soak in the fresh waters of God's pure and unconditional love.

Being with God

PONDERING

Allow the words of Isaiah to seep into your mind and heart:

"I have created you and formed you."

"Fear not, for I have redeemed you."

"I have called you by name."

"You are mine."

"You are precious in my eyes and glorious, and I love
 you."

Let God speak these loving words to you again and
again. Take one phrase each day and through it let God's
love penetrate your spirit and drench your heart. Let God
know how you feel as you allow God to speak these words
of love to you again and again.

SHARING

God my creator, your love is so abundant, life-giving,
nurturing. As I contemplate your love and let it encompass
my whole being, I feel humbled and grateful. I want to be
open to the breadth and length and height and depth of
your love for me. I ask you to remove from me whatever
blocks your love—feelings of unworthiness, my shame, my
fear of intimacy. Indeed, I am not worthy to receive your
unbounded love. But you look not at my sins but at my
desire for you. Give me the grace and the freedom to
respond to your desire to love me and transform me. Give
me a listening heart to hear you call me by name to experience your overflowing love.

LISTENING

*My child, from all eternity you were fashioned in my womb.
I tenderly held you in my womb until I was ready to birth you. I
created you and formed you and wrapped you in my love. Know
that my love surrounds you. My love is wrapped around you like*

clothing. I carry you in my arms. I hold you close to my heart. I nourish you at my breast. I love you more than you could ever imagine.

My beloved, know that the brilliant light of my love envelops you. Allow it to penetrate to the very core of your being. Allow my love to soak in, as the rays of the sun seep into the earth. The light of my love will burn away the darkness of your sinfulness. The penetrating strength of my love will redeem your brokenness. Be open to the purifying power of my love.

My precious one, allow the fresh water of my love to soak into your heart and spirit. Be like a sponge and allow the abundant waters of my grace to soak you through and through. Be an open vessel and receive the outpouring of my love. My love will then overflow into the lives of many around you. Just be still, open, and receptive.

RESPONDING

Find a picture of yourself when you were a baby or small child and let God speak the words from Isaiah to your little child during your prayer time.

Take a walk in the sun and feel the warmth of the sun penetrating your body. Let the warmth of the sun be God's tender love surrounding you.

The next time you take a bath or shower, be very attentive to the water flowing against your body and savor it as God's love soaking into your body, heart, and spirit.

God Molding Us

The Potter and the Clay

This word came to Jeremiah from the Lord: "Rise up, be off, to the potter's house; there I will give you my message." I went down to the potter's house and there he was working at the wheel. Whenever the object of clay which he was making turned out badly in his hand, he tried again, making the clay another object of whatever sort he pleased. Then the word of the Lord came to me. "Can I not do to you, house of Israel, as this potter has done? says the Lord. Indeed, like clay in the hand of the potter, so are you in my hand, house of Israel" (Jeremiah 18:1–6).
O Lord, you are our father; we are the clay and you are the potter: we are all the work of your hands (Isaiah 64:7).

Yahweh spoke to the Israelites very powerfully through the Old Testament prophets with the image of the potter and the clay. This creative image represents so beautifully our experience of God's intimate and intricate love.

It portrays three aspects, three seasons, of our spiritual growth: conversion, purification and transformation.

CONVERSION

As we journey through life, God calls us again and again to *conversion*. Sometimes this "change of heart" is rather dramatic and drastic, but many times it is quiet and somewhat unnoticed by others. Conversion is not only from sin to sinlessness, but also from mediocrity to greater holiness. As we live in relationship with God in our daily lives, then we experience from time to time a nudging from God to change—to enter more deeply into God's mind, heart, and life.

Jeremiah symbolizes this conversion experience in verse 4: "Whenever the object of clay which the potter was making turned out badly in his hand, he tried again making of the clay another object of whatever sort he pleased." Our God never gives up on us, but tries again and again. Our God continues to call us to conversion whenever we get into a rut, whenever our hearts of flesh become hearts of stone, and in whatever aspect of our lives that we are resisting God's shaping us. God untiringly molds us, forms us, into the vessel God wants us to be—a vessel representing the person of Jesus.

PURIFICATION

Hand in hand with the experience of conversion is the process of *purification*. As our hearts change and we begin to surrender to God's shaping us, we need to be purified in the more subtle, seemingly unknown areas of our hearts. God's grace penetrates the dark crevices of our being and brings them into the light. The process of purification can sometimes be painful as we become more deeply aware of our sinfulness and our need to be cleansed. However, when we are bathed in God's overflowing love and rooted deeply in God's gracious heart, then this process becomes a gentle, life-giving movement.

This experience of purification is portrayed by one of the steps of the potter forming the vessel. One time-consuming step is the potter working out the air bubbles in the clay. The potter spends hours, with his hands getting dirtier and dirtier, working out the impurities in the clay. The vessel must be free of all air bubbles for it to become a masterpiece. Our God acts the same way in us. God enters lovingly into the core of our sinfulness to work out all our impurities, all our "air bubbles." Truly, "we are the work of your hands."

TRANSFORMATION

As we become more and more purified, we enter deeply into the movement of *transformation*. Our darkness is transformed into light and our old self is changed into a new person. Through the purging of our sinfulness, we are transformed into the image of God's Son. By taking on the mind and heart of Christ, we enter more deeply into relationship with God, self, and others. The Word becomes enfleshed within us. The fruits of the Spirit come alive in us.

Just as the potter molds clay into a beautiful vessel and fires it into a shining masterpiece, so too God forms us into the image and likeness of Jesus, "in whom God is well-pleased" (Matthew 3:17). Jesus experienced the fullness of humanity. As we become a masterpiece in God's eyes, we grow in the fullness of our humanity and become God's greatest glory: persons fully alive in God.

CONCLUSION

These movements on our spiritual journey—conversion, purification and transformation—may occur in many ways and at different times in our lives. Various aspects of the vessel are being formed. These three aspects of our growth are continually taking place because we are always in process. We are in process until we die; then we become the perfect masterpiece that God has been shaping us to be. "Indeed, like clay in the hand of the potter, so are you in my hand, says the Lord."

Being with God

PONDERING

Look at the potter—is the potter male or female? young or old? See yourself as a piece of clay in the hands of the potter. Feel the potter's strong but gentle hands kneading the clay. Notice the single-hearted concentration of the potter. Feel the potter's reverence and love in holding the clay as it begins to take form.

Surrender to the touch of the potter. Feel the "air bubbles" of your sinfulness being worked out—your negative attitudes, resentments, fears. Feel the cleansing water that the potter uses to help the clay be even more pliable. Let yourself be molded into a beautiful vessel—one that will never be duplicated. Savor your own uniqueness and specialness. Notice the potter's look of delight and admiration.

SHARING

God of beauty, thank you for the gentle and loving way that you mold me into a beautiful masterpiece. Give me the grace to surrender to your loving touch. Give me the trust to know that you are doing all for my good, even the painful process of purification. You desire that I be pure and holy in your sight. Help me to be pliable and soft in your hands. Transform my hardened heart and mind. Mold me into the image and likeness of Jesus. Let the light of Jesus shine through my uniqueness and beauty.

LISTENING

My beautiful one, I hold you in the palm of my hands. I am molding you and transforming you into a beautiful creation. Put your trust in me. Even though you feel fragile inside at times, my strength is within you holding you together and forming you. Let me change your heart of stone into a heart of flesh—a heart that is loving, forgiving, and compassionate, like my heart. Surrender to my loving and warm touch. I am the master artist; you are my masterpiece. You are unique and beautiful in my sight.

RESPONDING

Pray with a piece of clay. Imagine God the potter holding it and looking at it. Let the potter form and re-form it each day to represent how your heart is. Let it reflect the attitudes and feelings of your mind and heart each day. Ask the potter to work out the "air bubbles" in you that are keeping you from being free and alive.

Find a beautiful glazed piece of pottery that represents yourself as God sees you. Keep it in a place where you can look at it each day. Be attentive to God's heart as you contemplate this piece of pottery. Let God reveal to you God's love and delight in you.

God has radically transformed great sinners into great saints. Pray this beautiful prayer of St. Augustine, asking God to mold you and transform you:

> Late have I loved you, O Beauty ever ancient, ever new, late have I loved you! You were within me, but I was outside, and it was there that I searched for you. In my unloveliness I plunged into the lovely things which you created. You were with me, but I was not with you. Created things kept me from you; yet if they had not been in you they would not have been at all. You called, you shouted, and you broke through my deafness. You flashed, you shone, and you dispelled my blindness. You breathed your fragrance on me; I drew in breath and now I pant for you. I have tasted you, now I hunger and thirst for more. You touched me, and I burned for your peace.

God Freeing Us

Circumcise Your Heart

> And now, Israel, what does the Lord your God ask of
> you but to fear the Lord your God, and follow God's
> ways exactly, to love and serve the Lord, your God,
> with all your heart and all your soul.... Think! The
> heavens belong to the Lord your God, as well as the
> earth and everything in it. Yet in God's love...the
> Lord was so attached so as to choose you. Circumcise
> your hearts, therefore, and be no longer stiff-necked.
> ...God executes justice for the orphan and the widow,
> and befriends aliens, feeding and clothing them. So
> you must befriend the alien (Deuteronomy10:12–20).

This passage from Deuteronomy describes the deepest desires of our heart. It states what God wants of us and
what we truly desire: "What does God ask of you?...to follow all God's ways, to love God, to serve God with all your
heart and all your soul..." (v. 12). What happens in us as we
strive to respond to God's desire to love us and our desire
to love God with all our hearts? We undergo a painful but

life-giving experience of the heart which has three move-ments: the movement of an obstinate heart, circumcised heart, and free heart.

OUR OBSTINATE HEART

Yahweh says: "Circumcise your heart, and be obsti-nate no longer" (v. 10). As we strive to let God circumcise our heart, free our heart, we often experience an unwant-ed resistance, a nagging obstinacy, a pervasive desire to run from God's touch. This can take the form of restless-ness in prayer, distractions, or an avoidance of a rumble beginning to take place in our heart.

This resistance often reveals the realness of our rela-tionship with God. Behind and underneath this resistance is a powerful grace about to emerge, a significant insight about ourselves or an encounter with God that's about to take place. This resistance can sometimes feel like a wall, or a shell covering over some deeper inner realities. It pro-tects us from feeling one or more of three strong feelings that need to be felt, shared with a spiritual director or trusted friend, and shared with God. These feelings are fear, unexpressed anger, or shame.

First, fear. As God begins to circumcise our heart, we can become fearful of God's closeness, the intensity of our own feelings, our pain and vulnerability. We might become fearful of losing control or of what God might ask of us. Our fear often has a hold on us rather than our deliberate-ly holding on to it. We do not want to be fearful: however, this unwanted fear suffocates our freedom.

Second, unexpressed anger. Resistance, or an obstinate heart, can also be a blanket covering over some unexpressed anger, such as an underlying rage at abuse experienced in childhood or an intense anger at being treated unjustly in a present situation. As we notice that our resistance blocks "unexposed anger," then "expressed anger" can emerge and become a powerful way to experience God. Because of God's loving presence and action within us, this unexpressed anger begins to bubble up, like black tar bubbling up in the heat of the sun. Our obstinacy is a way to run from our intense anger and rage, until we are ready to let it bubble over and share it with God and another person.

Third, shame. Resistance could be a protection from feeling some basic, toxic shame. If we let God circumcise our heart, we may begin to feel that we are defective persons unworthy of God's love and attention. We might feel: how could God possibly love me? how can I love me—such a fearful, angry, shame-filled person? Our toxic shame may be so great that we unknowingly feel that we will be annihilated if we let God come too close. Thus, our obstinate, running, stubborn, resistant heart is a protection which keeps us from feeling our deeper feelings, experiencing our basic woundedness as human beings, and experiencing God's love for us.

OUR CIRCUMCISED HEART

God, however, in God's great love sees through our walls and defenses. God's loving attention begins to penetrate our obstinate, resistant heart. Our heart begins to be circumcised, broken open, pierced as God holds us and loves us. As our resistance begins to crumble, we feel pain we never felt before. We get in touch with the depths of our fear, our terror. We begin to see how much we unknowingly hate ourselves and abuse ourselves. We feel the anger and rage we blocked off for so long. Our hearts of stone are becoming hearts of flesh. Our hardened hearts are softening. Our suffocated hearts are beginning to breathe deeply again. Our hearts are circumcised; they throb with pain. We discover that underneath our resistance and wall of denial is a throbbing, bleeding, and very human heart that God holds tenderly in God's loving hands. We feel pain we never felt before, but at least we are alive in our more authentic and deeper self. We will never be the same.

OUR FREE HEART

Why does God initiate and invite us to such a painful circumcision of heart? God circumcises our heart so that we may have a free heart—a heart that is wounded yet healed, weak yet strong, vulnerable yet alive, pierced yet joyful. God wants to give us a passionate heart that feels feelings and a compassionate heart that feels with, that "loves the stranger, the alien, the sojourner" (v. 19). God desires to give us an embracing heart that holds as precious the estranged parts of ourselves that we or others have abandoned or left out in the cold. God wants us to accept all dimensions of ourselves for our own well-being as well as others'. Through embracing our own fearful, angry, shameful selves, we will more compassionately embrace other broken and alienated persons—the poor, the homeless, the sick, the suffering. God desires to give us a heart that is open to God, full of feeling, overflowing with love for God, ourselves, and others.

CONCLUSION

Mechtild of Magdeburg, a twelfth-century mystic, says: "Whoever is sore wounded by love will never be made whole unless she embrace the very same love which wounded her." God's love wounds our hearts. It cuts through our defenses, penetrates our resistance, and embraces the alien parts of ourselves. The more deeply we let God's circumcising love penetrate and embrace our obstinate hearts, the more completely we are transformed into persons who are free and alive.

Being with God

PONDERING

Take a moment for contemplation. Open your hands on your lap. Imagine God's open hands gently holding your open hands. Place your heart in your hands and see it resting in yours and God's hands. What is your heart like at this moment? Is it obstinate and resistant with a shell or wall around it? Is it being circumcised at this moment—in pain, bleeding, being broken open? Or is it free and joyful today, beating with fullness of life? However your heart is, know that it is precious to God. God and you are holding it tenderly and lovingly. Ask God to reveal to you the deep feelings and reasons underneath the resistance. Accept your heart as it is with the confidence that God is transforming it. Thank God for the gift of your heart which allows you to be fully human. Offer your heart to God as the most important gift you have to give. As you and God tenderly hold your heart, pray for God's mercy and love to penetrate your heart more deeply.

SHARING

God of my heart, you desire to give me a passionate heart of love, but at times I run from my own feelings and your love. I ask you to touch my stoical heart to your passionate heart of love.

God of my desires, you desire to give me a soft heart, a heart of flesh, but at times my heart is stony. I ask you to penetrate my hardened heart with your compassionate heart of love.

God of my life, you desire to give me an embracing heart, but at times I run from my own vulnerability and the pain of others. I ask you to hold my fearful and closed heart to your heart of freedom and joy.

LISTENING

My beloved, your heart is a precious gift to me. I hold it lovingly in my hands. I gently massage those hardened and unfree places of your heart so your heart can be pliable, soft, and free. I tenderly embrace the shameful areas of your heart so they can be transformed into acceptance and joy. I lovingly hold the broken places of your heart so you can be made whole. I carefully circumcise your heart so that it can be one with my heart.

Let your heart rest in my hands so that I can transform it and renew it through my loving embrace.

RESPONDING

Take some clay and knead it to represent how your heart is today—obstinate, circumcised, free. Each day knead the clay into the way your heart feels. As you pray hold the clay which represents your heart that day; also, let God tenderly hold it. Notice if there are any changes in your heart as you pray and knead the clay accordingly.

When your heart is obstinate, write down in your journal the inner and outer realities that are causing it to be this way. Share with God these realities and be attentive to God's response.

God Becoming Enfleshed in Us

Pondering, Wrestling, Emptying

The Word became flesh and dwelt among us (John 1:14).

On our spiritual journey we daily invite God to be born anew within us. We strive to prepare a spacious dwelling place for God in our hearts. We enter into prayerful reflection on the word of God, asking God to be enfleshed in our lives. However, depending on the mood of our hearts and the circumstances of our lives, we approach God in various ways. As we strive to allow God's loving presence to be enfleshed in our hearts and lives, we might encounter God in a pondering, wrestling, or self-emptying stance. These three encounters are those of the three main characters of the first incarnation event—Mary, Joseph, and Jesus.

MARY PONDERING

As a very young woman, Mary receives a surprising call from God that will change the whole course of her life. As she accepts the angel's profound invitation to be the mother of God, she deeply ponders the meaning of this overwhelming experience during the nine months of her pregnancy. She turns these things over in her heart many times as she visits her cousin, Elizabeth, and prepares for the birth of the "Son of the Most High." She struggles with the ramifications of this invitation for the rest of her life.

One way we encounter God is that of *Mary pondering*. What does it mean to ponder in our hearts? It means reflecting on the events of our life in relation to our experience of faith. It involves dialoguing with God about questions such as: How are you present, God, in the events of my life? How are you revealing yourself to me today through the circumstances of the day? It means listening to the quiet stirrings of the Holy Spirit as experienced in the interior depths of our heart and the exterior breadth of our life. Pondering each day who God is for us and who we are before God, as Mary did, leads to a deeper knowledge of the incarnation: the Word becomes concretely *enfleshed* in our minds, hearts, and lives.

JOSEPH WRESTLING

This unexpected call to Mary understandably bewilders Joseph; it also will change the course of his life. Joseph, like Jacob in the Old Testament, wrestles with God about Mary's pregnancy. Understandably confused and deeply upset about this unexpected occurrence, he asks: Should I divorce Mary? How should I go about the divorce? Through prayerful wrestling with the Lord he comes to some degree of certainty that God's ways, which certainly are not his ways, are being manifested through these circumstances. With quiet trust and hopeful patience he waits for the full mystery of God's plan to be revealed.

At times in our lives, we encounter God like *Joseph wrestling*. We wrestle with God about realities we do not understand and find almost impossible to accept. Through avid prayer and struggling with God, our confusion and pain can be transformed into the acceptance and trust that Joseph experienced. Through much wrestling we come to see that "with God all things are possible" (Matthew 19:26). We then can wait upon the Lord with hopeful expectation that God's life will be *incarnated* in our human lives.

JESUS EMPTYING

By the Word becoming flesh, the utter poverty of God comes into focus: "...God emptied self and took the form of a slave, being born in the likeness of humanity" (Philippians 2:7). Jesus did not cling to divinity, but gave it up so that we could share in the divine life of God. Jesus chooses to be stripped of power and to become a weak, dependent baby. Stripped of everything, he becomes totally emptied for the sake of love.

On our journey with God we are invited into *Jesus' experience of self-emptying*. We are called to empty ourselves of all self-seeking in order to prepare a pure resting place for God in our hearts. We are prompted to let go of all those attitudes and things we cling to in our hearts, so that we can make room for the Living God in our lives. We experience our need for God. God gently encourages us to allow God to fill our emptiness, the void within us, with divine love and life. By giving everything we are and have to God in utter self-emptying as Jesus did, we prepare a dwelling place for Jesus. We invite him to be *born* in us.

CONCLUSION

Three different ways of encountering God...

—*pondering* the Word of God as manifested in the events of our life.

—*wrestling* with God as God reveals God's desires to us and incarnates divine life in us.

—being *poor and emptied* of all things to make room for God in the inn of our hearts.

God desires to become enfleshed within us. By pondering, wrestling, and emptying ourselves, we more readily can open ourselves to the profound experience of God becoming incarnate within us each day.

Being with God

PONDERING

Contemplate each person in this incarnation event. Imagine, relive, and enter into the experience of Mary, Joseph, and Jesus.

Ponder with Mary. Put yourself in her place and feel what she must have felt, possibly some fear and confusion coupled with trust and surrender to God.

Wrestle with Joseph. Be with him as he tosses around in bed trying to get to sleep, yet feeling so overwhelmed by this unexpected turn of events.

Empty yourself with Jesus totally emptied and poor. Feel his total dependence on Mary and Joseph. Let him share with you his love—he empties himself of divinity and becomes a dependent little baby for love of you.

Do any of your own experiences come to mind that are similar to those of these three persons? Do you relate to any one of the three experiences right now in your life more strongly than the other two? Are you Mary pondering? or Joseph wrestling? or Jesus being emptied? Share with God any feelings or concerns that arise in you, and be attentive to God's response.

SHARING

God of stillness, give me the gift of a contemplative mind and heart, so that I can ponder the various events of my life as Mary did. Help me to stop, look, and listen—to be attentive to your presence and actions in my heart and life. Give me the grace of a discerning heart so I can more readily discover your ways and your desires in my life circumstances.

God of struggle, your ways are not always easy to understand and accept. Give me the courage to wrestle with realities in my life that are confusing and unclear. Help me to be open to the surprising and unexpected events in my life. Give me the trust that Joseph gained through his wrestling with you.

God of emptiness, thank you for giving us such a beautiful example of poverty in Jesus. Help me to empty myself of all that is not you so I can make room in my heart for your love. Give me the insight to see that emptiness for you and in you is really fullness—in my emptiness you give me richness of life in Jesus. By becoming poor like Jesus I am gaining the greatest wealth—the fullness of your love. Give me the grace to be poor in spirit.

LISTENING

My faithful one, know that to enflesh me in your heart is not easy, to incarnate me in your life is a struggle. You must contemplate my loving presence, wrestle with my seeming paradoxes, and empty yourself of unnecessary realities and binding attitudes. In this way you will let me be born in your heart.

"My ways are not your ways, nor are my thoughts your thoughts" (Isaiah 55:8). You must ponder my ways and my thoughts so that my divine life can be enfleshed in your human life. Let yourself be surprised by my sometimes unexpected ways of doing things. Know that I do all for your good, and will never leave you to struggle alone. My love is faithful and true. Abide in my steadfast love, and you will incarnate my love in your life.

RESPONDING

Find ways to develop a more contemplative attitude toward your life circumstances. Ask Mary to help you to take suffcient time to notice God's presence and ponder God's movement in your heart and life.

Ask God for the courage to wrestle with realities in your life which you would rather not deal with and avoid.

Ask God to show you those attitudes and things that clutter your heart and life and keep you from making room for God.

God Challenging Us

Three Questions of Jesus

"Who do you say that I am?" (Mark 8:29)
"Do you know what I have done for you?" (John
13:12)
"Do you love me?" (John 21:16)

Jesus asked various questions in his life on many different occasions. His questions often took people by surprise and challenged them to reflect on God's truth and their own truth, or lack of it. Three questions Jesus asked his disciples on their journey with him can challenge us on our own spiritual journey: Who do you say that I am? Do you know what I have done for you? Do you love me? Reflecting on these questions can help us discover more about our own unique relationship with God and challenge us to respond more deeply to God's vibrant love for us.

WHO DO YOU SAY THAT I AM?

Jesus asks the first question as he is journeying with his disciples to the villages around Caesarea Philippi (Mark

8:27–30). Jesus has already spent many weeks and months preaching the good news and healing ill people. Many people are wondering who this person is. In the midst of this wondering, Jesus asks the disciples: "But who do you say that I am?"

The answer to this question is basic to our spiritual life; it reflects the realness of our faith and reveals our attitude toward God. Throughout scripture God is revealed to us as a God of love: "God is love and those who abide in love abide in God and God in them" (1 John 4:16). All other notions and images of God reflect this ultimate truth. In the Old Testament, for example, God says: "I have loved you with an everlasting love" (Jeremiah 31:3). "I have carved you on the palm of my hand" (Isaiah 49:15). God promises to bear us up on eagles' wings (Psalm 91:4). In the New Testament, Jesus says: "I am the Good Shepherd" (John 10:14); "I am the Bread of Life" (John 6:35); "I am the true Vine, you are the branches" (John 15:5); "I am the Light of the world"(John 12:46). These images are revelations of the basic truth that "God is Love."

"Who do you say that I am?" Jesus challenges us to reflect on such questions as: What is my image of God? relationship with God? How do I see God? as Father or Mother? as friend? as shepherd? as Spirit? as brother? Sometimes we may relate to God as our Father or Mother, sometimes as our brother in Jesus, sometimes as our strength in time of need. Has my idea of God and how I relate to God changed through the years? How is God being revealed to me now on my spiritual journey? Reflecting on these questions will enable us to experience God as a more vibrant part of our lives.

DO YOU KNOW WHAT I HAVE DONE FOR YOU?

Jesus asks the second question during the last supper after he washed the feet of his apostles: "Do you know what I have done for you?" (John 13:1–13). Through the symbolic action of washing their feet, Jesus sums up his actions for the past three years; that is, as he has served them and many others, they also must serve others. By this final symbolic action and this question, Jesus challenges his disciples to reflect on his love for them during their three years together.

Jesus challenges us to reflect also—reflect on the years we have walked with Jesus and to acknowledge the unique ways God has loved and gifted us. "Do you know what I have done for you?" Consider what God has done for us. God has given us faith as our sustaining meaning in life, hope in time of discouragement, love in time of loneliness, joy in time of sorrow, peace in time of hardship, and strength in time of need. Even trials and pain can be an ultimate blessing because of the goodness and love which can result from these; e.g., sickness and death can often bring people closer together, a family problem can sometimes bring someone back to faith in God.

The life of Jesus himself has been a blessing beyond compare. He shows us the way to God, he promises to send the Holy Spirit, he gives us his body and blood in the eucharist to sustain us on our journey. Ultimately Jesus lays down his life for us through his passion and death. He rises from the dead to give us new life. Indeed, our God is a gracious and giving God! Jesus invites us to appreciate and savor God's goodness to us through the question: "Do you know what I have done for you?" He encourages us to enflesh God's goodness through our own love for others in washing their feet.

DO YOU LOVE ME?

Jesus asks the third question after his resurrection (John 21:15-19). Having just eaten a fish dinner on the shore of the Sea of Tiberias, Jesus asks Peter three times: "Do you love me?" Each time Peter responds "yes," Jesus says to him: "Feed my lambs...Feed my sheep."

Jesus addresses this question to us also. Our "yes" to him can take two forms—loving him directly through prayer and loving him by loving others. First, we can express our love for him directly by offering our lives to God each day and by communicating with God in prayer. Prayer is a *relationship*. It is spending time with God, allowing God to love us and responding to God's love by giving ourselves in return. When we pray it means we take our relationship with God seriously. Prayer is *surrender*. It is a surrender of our whole self to God—heart, mind, soul, and body. Just as Mary surrenders her whole life to God when she says "yes" to the angel Gabriel, so also we are called to that same total surrender. Prayer is *communication*. It is conversing with God as we would with a friend, entrusting to God our concerns, burdens, and joys. It is expressing our love for God in heartfelt words and concrete deeds. Also, prayer is listening to God by being open to the inner movements of the Spirit. Thus, our answer to Jesus' question "Do you love me?" needs to be answered in our hearts and spirits through prayer.

The second way we answer this question is through deeds, by how we love one another. When Peter answers "yes" to that question, Jesus says to him: "Feed my lambs...Feed my sheep." We are called to do the same—to love one another as God has loved us. We are meant to wash one another's feet, to be sensitive and responsive to others' needs, to forgive those who hurt us. We are called to lay down our lives for others, to sacrifice for each other, to give to those in need—the poor, the lonely, the sick. In the first two questions, we are invited to look at who God is for us and reflect on how God has blessed us. Through this third question "Do you love me?" Jesus invites us to respond to God's loving presence and gracious gifts in our prayer and by our loving actions.

CONCLUSION

Three simple questions—simple yet challenging and essential to give meaning to our spiritual journey:
"Who do you say that I am?"
"Do you know what I have done for you?"
"Do you love me?"
We must reflect upon and respond to these three questions in order:
—to continually rediscover who God is for us;
—to be aware of and grateful for what God has done and is doing in our lives;
—to respond to God in our hearts through prayer and in our lives through giving to others.
Through continuous faithfulness to our responses to these questions, our lives will be more full, deep, and happy. We will be able to personify what St. Irenaeus said: "God's greatest glory is a person fully alive."

Being with God

PONDERING

Ponder each of these three questions in your heart:
"Who do you say that I am?" Look at God and let

God reveal Self to you at this moment. Who is God for you right now? How is God revealing Self to you now? How do you feel as you sit in God's revealed presence? Share with God how you feel. Be attentive to God's response.

"Do you know what I have done for you?" Contemplate your life and notice the many ways that God has loved you. In what specific ways has God gifted you? How has God washed your feet? Listen to God reveal to you the concrete ways that God has loved and served you. Share with God any interior reactions.

"Do you love me?" How are you letting God know of your love in your prayer and life? What are you surrendering to God? Do you surrender yourself to God each day? In what specific ways are you showing your love for others? helping others grow closer to God? relieving the suffering of others? Listen to God as God shares gratitude for your love for God and others.

SHARING

God of truth, you reveal yourself to me in many ways. You desire that I know the truth about who you are. Open my mind and heart to how you want to reveal yourself to me today. Let me be attentive to the unexpected and surprising ways you communicate your loving presence.

Giving God, you have blessed me in so many ways throughout my life. Your very nature is to give. Help me to know and appreciate your many gifts. Let me not take them for granted.

Overflowing God, you instruct us through Jesus: "What you have received as a gift, give as a gift" (Matthew 10:8b). As you have given much to me, you desire that I in turn give to others. Help me to love as you love. Help me to

wash the feet of others as you have washed mine. May I give
to others without counting the cost.

LISTENING

*My beloved friend, what is mine is yours and what is yours
is mine. My deep desire is that you grow in a deep knowledge of
me and my ways. I want us to be one as we bring my abundant
love to many. I want us to walk in the same footsteps as we care
for others. I desire that we share all, that we give all for the well-
being of many, that we have the same heartbeat of love.*

*Open your mind to a deeper knowledge of me. Let your
heart be surprised by the many spiritual gifts I give to you.
Through your open heart, let my compassionate love overflow
into the lives of many. Allow your weakness to be a vehicle for my
strength. Let the intimacy that we share be evident to all.*

RESPONDING

Write out your responses to the three questions of
Jesus in this reflection. Let your mind and heart be challenged and transformed through these questions.

Browse through the New Testament and write down
other questions that Jesus asked. Ponder one of these each
day. Stay with those questions which most engage your
heart.

God Groaning
Over Us

Jesus' Longing for Us to Know Him

Philip said to Jesus, "Lord, show us the Father and that will be enough for us." "Philip," Jesus replied, "after I have been with you all this time, you still do not know me? Whoever has seen me has seen the Father. How can you say, 'Show us the Father'? Do you not believe that I am in the Father and the Father is in me? The words I speak are not spoken of myself; it is the Father who lives in me accomplishing his works. Believe me that I am in the Father and the Father is in me, or else, believe because of the works I do. I solemnly assure you, the one who has faith in me will do the works I do, and greater far than these" (John 14:8–12).

As Jesus begins to share his heart with his apostles for the last time, he encourages them not to worry, to trust in him. He reminds them that he is leaving to prepare a place

for them; he will return to take them with him. Although
he asserts clearly that he is the Way, the Truth, and the
Life, and that to know him means to know the Father
(John 14:1–7), Philip still boldly requests: "Lord, show us
the Father and that will be enough for us." Jesus exasperat-
edly responds! "Philip, after I have been with you all this
time, you still do not know me?" For three years Philip and
the others journeyed with him, shared with him, lived with
him. And still they did not comprehend. We hear Jesus'
impatience; we understand his groaning heart: "Philip,
after I have been with you all this time, you still do not
know me?"

How deeply Jesus longs for his followers to know him!
Underneath his exasperation and groaning lies an
unquenchable yearning for his apostles, and us, to understand him truly as he is—as one with his Father, united so
completely they are inseparable. What precisely does Jesus
long for us to know about him and his Father? In this passage Jesus discloses three qualities of God's way of loving
that he wants us to understand: God's closeness, God's
laboring, and God's empowering.

GOD'S CLOSENESS

Jesus longs for us to know *how close God is to us*:
"Whoever has seen me has seen the Father." Before the
incarnation of the Son, the Jews were emphatically aware
of the transcendence of their God. With the coming of
Jesus, God is immanently enfleshed in our human experience, intimately enmeshed in our lives, and personally
dwelling in our hearts. Jesus shows us the Father who
resides with us in flesh and blood in his incarnate Son.
God desires to be involved with the pain, sorrow, joy, and
concerns of our lives. Yahweh craves to be Emmanuel:

God-with-us. Our God not only exists beyond, but also dwells with us in the circumstances of our lives and in the desires of our hearts. Jesus lived with us in the flesh for thirty years to reveal God's immanence to us. Indeed, Jesus longs for us to realize how intimately God is intertwined with us.

GOD'S LABORING

Jesus desires us to know that *God labors for us*. "...it is the Father who lives in me accomplishing his works." Our creator God does not merely watch creation evolve; God works and labors in its unfolding and growing process. In Jesus, our God struggles and exerts divine energy so that we and all creation can thrive and flourish. Our God is not only a serene and quiet God; God also selflessly and actively toils for the fulfillment of creation.

God labors for us not only in creation but also in redemption. As Ignatius indicates in his "Contemplation on the Love of God": "God loves me so much that he enters into the very struggle of life: like a potter with clay, like a mother in childbirth, or like a mighty force blowing life into dead bones. God labors to share his life and his love. His labors take him even to death on a cross to bring forth the life of the resurrection." Jesus concretizes and lives out the creator's labor of love, especially through his passion and death. God's laboring gives birth to new life in the risen Lord.

GOD'S EMPOWERING

Jesus yearns for us to understand that *God empowers us*: "The one who has faith in me will do the works I do, and far greater than these." God's ongoing involvement is manifested through our self-giving. Jesus makes visible a God who continues to transform the world through our work, who accomplishes his tasks by the sharing of our gifts with each other. Through our growing faith and maturing trust, God's empowering comes to fruition in us. God completes the divine labor of love through us.

This faith is reciprocal: not only do we have faith in God, but God also has faith in us. Our trust in God as well as God's confidence in our ability and giftedness empowers us. We enter a mutual undertaking with our God to finish the redemption already accomplished in Jesus. God needs our gifts and abilities to complete in time what has taken place in eternity, and in a moment of time in Jesus' death and resurrection.

As Jesus departs from supper with his close friends, his longing for us to know him culminates in his death and resurrection. He manifests a knowledge rooted in passionate love and overflowing into total self-giving. He reveals a God who loves intensely with a love that is vulnerable and suffers because of its intensity. He discloses a God wounded by caring, wounds that continue to be open and painful. He makes visible a God deeply affected by us, who not only sheds tears but also sheds blood for us. In Jesus, then, we experience our God loving, not in a detached way, but in a totally involved and self-emptying way.

CONCLUSION

We hear God groaning over us in Jesus' yearning for us to know his heart. Jesus longs for us to understand our living God: an immanent God who is one with us in an intimacy beyond anything we could ask for or imagine; an involved God who labors and struggles for us in the unfolding of creation and redemption; an empowering creator who enables us to continue God's laboring through our self-giving; a passionate God who loves so intensely that the divine heart weeps and bleeds for us.

Jesus' longing explains his exasperation: "After I have been with you all this time, you still do not know me?" He continues to yearn that we journey beyond our existing knowledge of God and enter into the deep recesses of God's heart, where the fullness of our understanding of God is found.

Being with God

PONDERING

According to scripture, to "know" someone is to be intimate with them. Knowing God means having a heart-felt understanding of God. It implies a closeness, not just "knowing about" but knowing God in the depths of our being.

Reflect on your knowledge of God. What kind of knowledge is it? a head knowledge? a heart knowledge? Do you know truths about God or do you know God in an intimate relational way?

Ponder Jesus' desire for you to know him. How do you feel about his strong and groaning desire? Share with Jesus your feelings about his earnest desire.

SHARING

God of longing, you desire that I know you in my heart as well as in my mind. You want to share with me all the secrets of your heart. Open my mind and my heart to a deeper understanding of you. Help me to know the varied ways that you reveal yourself to me.

God of passion, your groaning reveals the deep and passionate love of your heart. Fill me with a passionate desire to know you.

God of transparency, your presence is so simple and pure that when we see Jesus we also see the Father and the Spirit. Help me to keep the eyes of my heart fixed on you and the many ways you reveal yourself.

LISTENING

My intimate one, know that I reveal the deepest secrets of my heart to those who are my most intimate followers. I am drawing you into the deeper recesses of my heart. Know that to see one of my faces is to see all of my faces, because my one face is love. Empty your mind and heart of all things, so that you can receive all–an empowering and life-giving knowledge of me. Stay close to my heart and you will never be disappointed.

RESPONDING

"Be still and know that I am God." Quiet your mind and heart, so you can hear God's simple word of love spoken to you today.

Spend time contemplating Jesus in the scriptures, because in coming to know him you are coming to know the many revelations of God's everlasting love.

Help others to come to know God through your love and your example of caring and reaching out to others.

God Strengthening Us

When I Am Weak, Then I Am Strong

"My grace is enough for you, for in weakness power reaches perfection." And so I willingly boast of my weakness instead, that the power of Christ may rest upon me....For when I am powerless, it is then that I am strong (2 Corinthians 12:9–10).

Peter experiences in his life two profound moments—one of weakness and one of power. He struggles with the agony and ecstasy of love and what it means to be human. A "no" shouted out in fear and weakness is transformed into a "yes" because of the love of Another. The experience of being broken changes a blind and self-satisfied heart into a vulnerable and compassionate heart.

Two encounters in the life of Peter—one of weakness and the other of power—also reveal these two dynamic moments in our own lives. Through contemplating two significant events in the life of Peter, we can ponder the value and meaning of our own experience of weakness and vulnerability.

"THE LORD TURNED AROUND AND LOOKED AT PETER" (Luke 22:61)

Jesus eats his last Passover meal with his apostles and friends, something which he longed to do. He washes their feet. Peter, again in his stance of thickheadedness and blindheartedness, emphatically blurts out: "You will never wash my feet" (John 13:8). Once again, the Lord gently and firmly puts Peter in his place.

A growing intensity of anguish and fear begins to overshadow Jesus. He arises and goes out to be with his Father in the garden. Anguish and fear overwhelm his being. Struggle and pain rip his heart raw to the point of shedding drops of blood. His exhausted friends sleep soundly at a distance.

Then it happens—his hour has come. Jesus is arrested, bound and carried off like a common criminal. The reality of Jesus' words begins to penetrate the heart and mind of Peter. He becomes overwhelmed with fear; yet in his love for Jesus, he follows him "at a distance" (Luke 22:54). Now the moment is upon Peter when he experiences the depths of his weakness and powerlessness. He denies the person he loves most in this world: "I do not know who you are talking about" (Luke 22:61). Professing to be strong and faithful to the end, he is thrown into the excruciating depths of his own weakness and faithlessness. His whole life crashes in on him.

Peter's agony, in a courtyard rather than in a garden, takes place: "The Lord turned around and looked at Peter." This look of Jesus tears Peter to pieces: "He went out and wept bitterly" (Luke 22:62). He is broken to the core of his being. The reality and truth of his own weakness overcome him. Because he loves Jesus so deeply, the intensity of pain is more than he can bear. The "thorn in his flesh"—his pride and fear—comes to light with excruciating intensity. What is in this look of Jesus that leads Peter to the stark truth of himself? Perhaps disappointment, hurt, desolation, fear. Perhaps also a great deal of love, understanding, and reassurance: "Now you know, Peter, what it is like to be weak. Now you know that you don't have it all together."

The scenario continues. A God and King who is proclaimed to be all-powerful enters into one of the most horrible displays of powerlessness in the history of humanity. "Why don't you come down from your cross? There is still time to show your power," is the attitude of many. But no; Jesus becomes weaker and weaker until he dies.

Peter is left behind, overwhelmed with the deep realization that he has failed his Lord and friend in time of need. Completely broken, he is kept alive by that last look of the Lord. Something in that brief glance sparks a dim ray of hope in Peter. Knowing he was not faithful to the Lord in life, he faintly hopes that he will be faithful to him in death. This time Peter, brought to the depths of his weakness, does not jump ahead of the Lord. He waits.

"SIMON, SON OF JOHN, DO YOU LOVE ME?"
(John 21:17)

"I have seen the Lord!" proclaims Mary Magdalene to Peter and the other disciples (John 20:13). The faint ray of hope in Peter's heart begins to become brighter—could Jesus really be alive? By appearing to him and others, the Lord gently and firmly builds up Peter's confidence and trust.

The risen Lord, fully human and alive, prepares a meal for Peter and the others by the Sea of Tiberias. Through a display of love and power in letting them catch a huge number of fish, Jesus renews their trust in him. Through a mundane and homey preparing of a meal, Jesus revitalizes their security and joy in the warmth of his love.

Then again Jesus looks at Peter: "Simon, son of John, do you love me?" Three times the same question; three times Peter's love for Jesus burns within him. In his vulnerability Peter begins to be transformed. Because of Jesus' love and confidence in him, Peter's weakness is transformed into power—not a power that is overbearing and prideful, but a power to love. "Feed my lambs; feed my sheep" (John 21:15,17). Because he experiences the depths of his weakness and the transforming power of God's love, Peter is ready now to serve others as Jesus does—with a compassionate heart. Peter's heart, torn apart and broken, now could be vulnerable and accepting of the weaknesses and sufferings of others. "Upon this rock I will build my church" (Matthew 16:18). Now Peter is that rock: not a rock of personal strength, but one of weakness and brokenness that can allow God's strength and love to come to perfection. In these two events, therefore, Peter dramatically lives out the experience of "when I am powerless, it is then that I am strong" (2 Corinthians 12:10).

THE VALUE OF WEAKNESS IN OUR LIVES

How many times we avoid weakness in our lives! How often we strive to be strong so no one will see our inner helplessness and powerlessness! For us to face our vulnerability is truly difficult. Like Peter, we become overwhelmed when faced with the naked truth of our inner poverty. Yet, by walking through Peter's experience and reflecting on our own, possibly the devastation of our weakness can be one of the richest experiences of our lives.

What possible value can facing our vulnerability have? One important outcome is that we discover the truth about ourselves. Powerlessness breaks us open, and we encounter the stark reality of our existence; that is, our very breath and life depends upon God alone. We are thrust into our own inner poverty so that all we can do is keep our eyes and heart on the Lord. We learn that: "In him I have strength for everything" (Philippians 4:13), which was Peter's experience. His weakness broke open his heart of pride and self-righteousness, his need to have everything under control. In the depths of his inner poverty, all he could hope for was that the look of the Lord in the courtyard would eventually change his total emptiness into fullness.

Through our experience of weakness we are instilled with the capacity to serve with a compassionate heart. Our ability to enter into the pain and weakness of another is enhanced. By our growing vulnerability we allow our hearts to be touched deeply by the suffering of another. We become less judgmental and more accepting of others' shortcomings and faults, because we have experienced our own. It was Peter's experience of his weakness that prepared him to be the compassionate foundation, the caring rock, of the church. Rooted in God's power and strength, Peter now could freely give himself—the self that was transformed by grace and love. He could let the light of the broken and risen Lord shine through him in his empathetic service of others.

Possibly the most profound value of our experience of weakness is that it engages us in a deeper and richer experience of God. We discover more completely a God who became powerless and weak, a God who was emptied of everything in order to become like us in all things. We experience a God who chose to be broken, to die a horrendous death, in order to show us the true meaning of life: it is not the love of power but the power to love that is the foundation of our call to be human. How deeply moving it is to have a God who shares our weakness, who taught us how to live joyfully and freely in poverty and powerlessness! What an overwhelming mystery to be loved by a God who became totally weak in the face of evil in order to confound the strong! Peter struggled to understand this paradoxical truth. How could his Lord and master talk about dying on a cross? How could such a powerful God choose to undergo such a tragic death? Again, through the experience of failure and weakness—his own and Jesus'—Peter learned the true nature of God. He discovered a God who is passionately in love with us and deeply desirous to be one with us in all things—the agony as well as the ecstasy of being human.

CONCLUSION

We have a choice. We can allow our weakness to harden and destroy our humanness, or we can let it empower us and move us into a fuller and richer experience of ourselves, others, and God. In choosing the latter, the Lord's words to Paul can become a consolation and a lived experience: "My grace is enough for you, for in weakness power reaches perfection."

Being with God

PONDERING

Prayerfully reflect on these questions: How have I reacted to experiences of weakness and vulnerability in my

life? Have I responded with the despair and discouragement of Judas, or with the unfailing trust of Peter in the
Lord's look of love? Does my own inner weakness and inse-
curity lead me to hardheartedness and closeheartedness,
or does it bring me to greater compassion and vulnerability? Be attentive to God's presence as you reflect and share.
Listen to how God desires you to let your weakness and
brokenness manifest the power of divine love.

SHARING

God of weakness, let my vulnerability become a resting place for you rather than a way to avoid you.

God of power, transform my weakness through the
power of your love. May the power of your love come alive
in my weakness.

God of strength, build up your strength within me
and complete the work of transformation you have begun
in me.

LISTENING

*My beloved, know that I love you as you are. Do not be con-
cerned with your weaknesses and failings. Your sins are washed
away and I make you as white and pure as snow. I am at the
very center of your being and in the depths of your weakness giving you my strength. Know how close I am to you. Know that my
love envelops you and transforms your vulnerability into my
strength. Do not look at your weaknesses and shortcomings, but
look at my power and mercy. Allow yourself to be broken as I was
broken, because in that way the power of my love can grow in
you more and more. My love is melting you, transforming you,
empowering you. Allow that to happen. I hold you close to my
heart. I am closer to you than you are to yourself.*

RESPONDING

One definition of prayer is: "Looking at God looking at you." As Jesus turned around and looked at Peter, notice how God looks at you with deep love and total acceptance. Notice the reverent look in God's eyes—God holds as sacred your weakness as well as your strength. Let God know the feelings that arise within you as you pay attention to God's accepting and reverent look.

Think of someone in your life right now of whose weaknesses you are particularly aware, someone who might be irritating you or whom you resent. Look at that person through the loving and accepting eyes of God. Ask God to help you to accept and reverence him or her as God does.

God Bearing Fruit in Us

Joy: The Fruit of Suffering

"I tell you truly, you will weep and mourn while the world rejoices; you will grieve for a time, but your grief will be turned into joy" (John 16:20).

Jesus says in the sermon on the mount: "Any sound tree bears good fruit, while a decayed tree bears bad fruit...by your fruits you will know them." One lively "fruit" that grows on the tree of our life as we journey with God is the fruit, or gift, of joy, "the joy that comes from the Holy Spirit" (1 Thessalonians 1:6). The joy of the Holy Spirit is a permeating quality of our lives when we strive to be open to God's loving presence. This joy is tinged with pain as our hearts grow more in union with God's heart. The paschal mystery becomes more of a reality in our lives the more deeply we live in God. However, the deeper and more intensely we suffer with Jesus, the deeper and more permeating will be our joy. The greater our willingness to sacrifice for God and God's people, the greater will be our experience of God's joy. Jesus' words to his closest friends at the last supper are spoken to us: "I tell you truly, you will weep and mourn while the world rejoices; you will grieve for a time, but your grief will be turned into joy" (John 16:20).

JESUS BORN IN JOY

Jesus' life on earth begins in joy and ends in joy. The angel says to Zechariah about the birth of John: "Joy and gladness will be yours, and many will rejoice at his birth" (Luke 1:14). A little while later the angel appears to Mary at the announcement of Jesus' coming birth, and says: "Rejoice, O highly favored daughter! The Lord is with you" (Luke 1:28). When Mary goes to visit Elizabeth, Elizabeth, filled with the Holy Spirit, exclaims: "Blest are you among women...the moment your greeting sounded in my ears, the baby leapt in my womb for joy" (Luke 1:42a, 44). Then Mary prays with joy and praise: "My being proclaims the greatness of the Lord, my spirit finds joy in God my savior" (Luke 1:46–47). Such tremendous joy filled the hearts of Mary and Elizabeth at these moments of salvation history!

But their joy would only be complete after enduring much suffering by accepting God's desires. Mary ponders deeply the words of Simeon the prophet: "This child is destined to be the downfall and the rise of many, a sign that will be opposed—and you yourself shall be pierced with a sword...(Luke 2:34–35a). At the birth of Jesus, there is great rejoicing among the angels and shepherds of Bethlehem, yet a little while later Mary and Joseph are forced to leave their country for a few years to protect the life of their infant son. However, they continue to respond to God's desires for them, which is their deepest joy even in the midst of turmoil and pain.

JESUS' JOY IN LIVING AND PREACHING

The story of Jesus' life continues. He proclaims the kingdom of God to all and tells his followers that their greatest joy is to share in this kingdom. He begins his great sermon on the mount with the beatitudes, which describe the great joys and blessings experienced by those who are willing to be poor and simple, and to suffer a little while for him and with him: "Happy are the poor in spirit, the reign of God is theirs....Happy are you when they insult you and persecute you and utter every kind of slander against you because of me. *Be glad and rejoice*, for your reward is great in heaven" (Matthew 5:3, 11–12).

Jesus labors day and night to proclaim the good news to the people, yet always takes time to experience simple human joys, such as the intimate moments of relaxation and fun he had with his disciples during the wedding feast of Cana and the celebration of the Jewish feast days. He knows, appreciates and celebrates the many human joys that are within everyone's reach.

The depth of Jesus' interior life does not dampen his practical attitude, but rather enhances his sensitivity to the mundane. He admires the birds of heaven, the lilies of the field. He celebrates the joy of the sower and the harvester, the happiness of the person who finds a hidden treasure, the joy of the shepherd who recovers his sheep or of the woman who finds her lost coin, the excitement of those invited to the feast, and the joy of the father who embraces his son returning from a prodigal life. For Jesus, these joys are real because for him they are signs of the spiritual joys of the kingdom of God: the joy of people who enter this kingdom, the joy of a loving God who welcomes them. His happiness is above all to see the word accepted, the possessed delivered, a sinful woman or a publican like Zacchaeus converted, a widow giving her last two pennies. He even exults with gladness: "I offer you praise, O Father, Lord of heaven and earth, because what you have hidden from the learned and clever you have revealed to the merest children" (Luke 10:21).

Yes, because Jesus is "a person like us in all things but sin" (Hebrews 4:15), he accepts and experiences human and spiritual joys as a gift from God. And he does not rest until "to the poor he proclaims the good news of salvation...and to those in sorrow, joy" (Luke 4:18). The gospel of Luke particularly gives witness to this seed of joy. The miracles of Jesus and his words of pardon are so many signs of divine goodness: "All the people rejoiced at all the glorious things that were done by him, and gave glory to God" (cf. Luke 13:17). Jesus lives a life of praise and thanksgiving to God for the many joys that the creator gives him.

JESUS' JOY IN GIVING HIS LIFE

Jesus' joy, however, would not be complete until he endured the greatest sacrifice of his life—laying down his life for his friends. At the last supper Jesus reveals the fullest and deepest meaning of joy—*joy experienced because of the suffering that comes with loving*. The source of his joy is his intimate union with the Father. He shares with his apostles, his friends, the deepest truths of his heart, which are there because he is one with the Father. He shows them that their greatest joy will be like his—being united to the Father and to one another; being willing to lay down their lives for each other.

Jesus tells the apostles that their greatest experience of joy will come after they suffer for a while, after they grieve for a time:

> I tell you truly: you will weep and mourn while the world rejoices; you will grieve for a time, but your grief will be turned into joy. When a woman is in labor, she is sad that her time has come. When she has borne a child, she no longer remembers her pain for joy that a person has been born into the world.
> In the same way, you are sad for a time, but I shall see you again; then your hearts will rejoice with a joy no one can take from you (John 16:20–22).

Jesus explains that the full meaning of his death and resurrection and the transformation of suffering into joy would take place through the power of the Holy Spirit: "This much have I told you while I was with you; the Paraclete, the Holy Spirit whom the Father will send in my name, will instruct you in everything, and remind you of all that I told you" (John 14:25–26). It is through the Holy Spirit that the reality of the paschal mystery becomes clear. It is through the Holy Spirit that God's love, strength, and joy are given: "Ask and you shall receive, that your joy may be full" (John 16:24).

OUR JOY IN SUFFERING WITH JESUS

By sharing in the suffering of the passion and death of Jesus, we will be able to share in the happiness of his resurrection, his most profound experience of joy. The apostles develop this truth in their epistles. Peter says:

> Do not be surprised, beloved, that this fiery ordeal should have befallen you, to test your quality; there is

nothing strange in what is happening to you. Rather
rejoice, when you share in some measure the sufferings of Christ. When his glory is revealed, you will
rejoice exultantly (1 Peter 4:12–13).

James states: "Consider yourselves *happy* indeed, my
brethren, when you encounter trials of every sort" (James
1:2).

Paul says that through endurance we are purified
and experience the joy and hope of attaining glory. In
Paul "being confident" is equivalent to "rejoice." So Paul
says to be "confident," that is, "joyful" over our afflic-
tions, because "affliction gives rise to endurance, and
endurance gives proof of our faith, and a proved faith
gives ground for hope. And this hope will not leave us
disappointed, because the love of God has been poured
out in our hearts through the Holy Spirit" (Romans 5:
3–5).

Therefore, by sharing in the death and resurrection
of Jesus, we experience the deepest joy, a joy no one can
take away from us. We experience the power of the Holy
Spirit in the paradox of our Christian faith: neither trials
nor sufferings have been eliminated from this world, but
they take on new meaning in the certainty of sharing in
the redemption and glory of Jesus. This is why we,
though struggling with the challenges of human life, do
not need to grope for the way. Nor do we see in death
the end of our hope. As the prophet foretold: "The people that walked in darkness have seen a great light; on
those who live in a land of deep shadow a light has
shone. You have made their gladness greater, you have
made their joy increase" (Isaiah 9:1–2).

CONCLUSION

Jesus' joy becomes complete when he submits to his death for love of us. He is stripped of everything and empties himself in order to give us everything. Through his death and resurrection he changes our sorrow and distress into joy. He shows us the meaning of the words: "By your fruits you will know them." By the experience of enduring and suffering with Jesus, God brings to fruition true and lasting joy—a joy that no one can take from us. Hannah Hurnard in her book *Mountain of Spices* sums up very beautifully some of the thoughts of this truth that deep joy is the fruit of suffering:

> Hark to Love's triumphant shout!
> > "Joy is born from pain,
> Joy is sorrow inside out,
> > Grief remade again.
> Broken hearts look up and see
> This is love's own victory."
>
> Here marred things are made anew,
> > Filth is here made clean,
> Here are robes, not rags, for you,
> > Joy where tears have been.
> Where sin's dreadful power was found,
> Grace doth now much more abound.
>
> Hark! such songs of jubilation!
> > Every creature sings,
> Great the joy of every nation,
> > "Love is King of Kings.
> See ye blind ones! shout, ye dumb!
> Joy is sorrow overcome."

As we continue our journey with God, may we ask the

Holy Spirit to help us experience God's joy even in the midst of deep pain.

Being with God

PONDERING

Contemplate the many human and spiritual joys that have been part of your life. Write them down in your journal. Savor each joy as you contemplate it, no matter how small or large.

Contemplate in particular the joys that have been couched in suffering and pain. Write these down and notice how you feel as you ponder them. Share with God your feelings.

SHARING

God of joy, thank you for letting me experience the gift of joy in my heart. Thank you for the many joys that have entered my life. Help me to hold each joy as precious.

God of pain, you showed me how to experience joy even in the midst of deep suffering. Thank you for letting me suffer with you. Give me the joy of the Holy Spirit, the deep joy that no one can take away from me, the joy of total union with you.

LISTENING

My beloved, know that I am with you always. Put your total trust in me. I take care of all. You do not understand the suffering and pain of humanity or of yourself, but one day you will understand. One day you will understand that through your suffering I am forming you into a beautiful masterpiece. One day you will know what love really is—my way of loving. My way is different from yours. My way involves the cross, a stripping, an emptying. Can you not see how I loved? Can you not see how I suffered the loss of everything, my divinity when I became human, and my humanity when I died on the cross, in order to love you totally and to give you lasting joy?

I invite you into my way of loving. I invite you to be broken and bleeding and wounded as I was. You will rejoice because of your brokenness. Your love will be perfect because of your wounds. My wounds and your wounds will make you free. Allow me to mold you and fashion you in your brokenness and woundedness. Then you will experience the deepest joy that no one can take away from you.

RESPONDING

Let the warmth of God's joy permeate the rawness of your wounds. Wrap a blanket around yourself as a gesture of God's joy enveloping your vulnerability and brokenness. Feel the warmth of that blanket and bask in God's loving presence.

Share with someone a painful experience in which you experienced joy in the midst of pain. Notice how you feel as you share that experience.

God Permeating Our Lives

Life: A Mystery To Be Lived?
Or a Problem To Be Solved?

Jesus said, "Do not worry about your livelihood, what you are to eat or drink or use for clothing. Is not life more important than food? Is not the body more valuable than clothes? Look at the birds in the sky. They do not sow or reap, they gather nothing into barns; yet your heavenly Father feeds them. Are not you more important than they? Which of you by worrying can add a moment to your life-span?
...Stop worrying then over questions like, 'What are we to eat, or what are we to drink, or what are we to wear?' Your heavenly Father knows what you need.
Seek first God's kingdom and way of holiness and all these things shall be yours as well" (Matthew 6:25–33).

These familiar and seemingly simple words of Jesus offer us an ideal which is challenging, subtle, and timely. These words are challenging because Jesus offers an important choice, and serious decisions are rarely easy to make. They are subtle because they deal with deeper attitudes of our hearts and minds. They are timely because they represent the atmosphere in which we live today.

Jesus says, "Seek first God's kingdom and God's holiness and all these things shall be yours as well." Yet we live in an age of economic crisis in which worry and anxiety are the common attitudes on both a national and personal level. How many of us have been concerned and anxious about the cost of living, the rising interest rates, or the possibility of losing our jobs? We all worry about economic realities to some degree. Does this mean Jesus' words are irrelevant?

Jesus says, "Do not be anxious about *things*—food, drink, and clothing," yet these things are an essential part of our lives, things which we could not survive without. Concern about these necessities of life can affect our whole outlook on life—life can become a series of problems to be solved, rather than a mystery to be lived. We can get bogged down in our many concerns. We can lose sight of the real meaning of life. Our priorities can get mixed up. Does this mean Jesus' words are unrealistic?

This reflection explores the truth that not only is it *possible* to live life as a mystery rather than as a series of problems to be solved, but that it is *essential* to live this kind of life if we are going to be true followers of Jesus Christ and live full and happy lives. Two experiences are described which personify the two contrasting attitudes which Jesus presents in this teaching from the sermon on the mount—that of trust in God as opposed to overanxiety. These experiences of a married couple and a married woman represent two alternatives of how to view and live life—as a mystery or as a problem. Then three principles are explored which can help us experience life more fully.

TWO EXPERIENCES

Tina and Bob are a young couple with a newborn baby boy who recently moved into a new apartment complex. Not having an abundance of money, like many young couples beginning a new life together, they both work very hard to make ends meet and to live a happy life together. One day they had a terrible experience! Because of improper construction of the sewerage system, they were invaded by rats—three or four of the worst kind! Who would ever think in a nice area of town in a new apartment that rats would appear! Tina and Bob certainly did not.

Tina and Bob's outlook on this dreadful invasion of rats, as their whole outlook on life, made the ideal which Jesus presents a living reality. Although they were very worried about where or how they were going to move and deeply worried about their baby son, their trust in God went deeper than their worry. They were so thankful to God for protecting their baby son and themselves from harm. Their "life" and their "bodies," as Jesus suggests, were more important than food and shelter. Although Tina and Bob had a serious problem to face at the moment, their outlook on life was that life was a gift from God, and therefore a mystery to be lived rather than a problem to be solved. They were able to cope with this particular problem because of their underlying view of life— they put God first and trusted that God would take care of all their needs. Tina explained that this crisis could have overwhelmed them, especially since financially they were just about making it anyway, except that they knew that

God had never let them down before and they believed God would not allow them to sink this time. In short, they had real reason to become bogged down in worry, yet they trusted.

The second story is about a married woman, Marie. Marie has four children, a nice home, a good husband who is making a sufficient amount of money to put their four children through college. Marie is suffering. She is suffering because of her over-anxious and unnecessary concern about their children, their education, and her future life without them around the house. She has been suffering from colitis and arthritis for years which she realizes is partly a result of her excessive worry.

Marie, by all appearances, is a cheerful, happy, person, but in reality worries about so many things. She realizes that instead of thanking God for the many blessings she has, she becomes over-anxious about what she may not have in the future. She has forgotten that her "life" and her "body," as Jesus says, are of greater importance than external concerns. She realizes she needs spiritual help to put first things first and to live a full and happy life—to view life as an unfolding mystery to be lived, not a problem to be solved.

On our own spiritual journey, we can probably relate to both Tina and Bob's experience of trust and Marie's experience of anxiety. We have possibly experienced both inner realities. How can we see life more as a mystery to be lived rather than as a problem to be solved? How can we enflesh the ideal Jesus places before us to have God first in our lives and to believe God will give us everything we need? The following three principles can help us in this endeavor.

FIRST THINGS FIRST

The first principle to help us to live life in its beauty and fullness rather than to live it as a series of problems is to put *first things first,* and to examine ourselves frequently to be sure our priorities are in right order. This is what Jesus means when he says: "Seek first God's kingdom and God's way of holiness." We must examine ourselves daily to see in what order our values and concerns are. In what order does Jesus say these should be? He says that concern for the things of God—God's kingdom and a holy life—must come first. The less important concerns of life, which at times seem overwhelming to us, will eventually be worked out because they are in their proper perspective.

Viktor Frankl, a physician who suffered untold persecution in Germany during the Nazi regime, came to this profound conclusion about life. He says: "Anyone who has a *why* to live for can live with almost any *how*." In other words, if we have found deep meaning to sustain our lives, according to Frankl, we can handle any burden, any concern, any worry, that comes our way. Isn't that what Jesus is suggesting? If we find our deepest and primary meaning in God, if God and God's kingdom come first, than we will be able to deal with any crisis that comes our way and not become overly concerned about our physical needs.

Teresa of Avila, a religious who lived during the sixteenth century who founded and reformed many convents during her lifetime, says it another way:

> Let nothing disturb thee.
>> Let nothing affright thee.
> All things are passing;
>> God only is changeless.
> Patience gains all things
>> Who hath God wanteth nothing.
> God alone sufficeth.

Are we able to say "God alone sufficeth," that "all things are passing," that "patience gains all things"? If we can say these things then we can thank God for helping us to put God first in our lives. If these truths are not our lived realities, then we need to examine ourselves and see why they are not. We need to ask God daily to help us to put first things first and to have God's perspective on life.

TRUST IN GOD

A second principle that enables us to experience the fullness of the mystery of life is to *trust in God* for all of our needs. Jesus says, "Your heavenly Father knows that you need them all." God wants to give us so much; however, we need to trust. God has given us life, and if God has given us life then we can trust God for the lesser things.

In the Old Testament Yahweh says through the prophet Isaiah, "See! I will not forget you....I have carved you on the palm of my hand" (Isaiah 49:16). Do we have this kind of trust—to believe that we are in God's hand, to trust that God will never let us sink? Or on the other hand, can we relate more to Jesus' words: "O you of little faith!"

Also, in the Old Testament we have such a beautiful example of trust as represented by Abraham (Genesis 22:1–18). Abraham trusted God enough to allow himself to be led from the familiarity and comforts of his own land to a new destination. He trusted enough to know that God would even use the sacrifice of Isaac, something which Abraham did not understand at all, to accomplish the divine purposes. Because Abraham trusted so completely in God, the mystery of his life began to unfold and he experienced the fullness and beauty of life. Again, God's kingdom and way of holiness came first, and therefore all else was given to him besides. God gave back to Abraham his son Isaac and made Abraham the father of all lands because he gave up his own land. Yes, Abraham put God first in his life and trusted in God for everything.

PRAY ALWAYS

A third principle to help our life to be the fullness of a mystery to be lived rather than a series of problems to be solved is to *develop a life of prayer*. When we pray we are not merely "saying prayers," but communicating with God in a personal way so that we can see things with God's eyes and so that our ways become more and more God's ways. Developing a life of prayer makes the first two principles somewhat easier. Through prayer we develop an attitude of putting God's kingdom first; through prayer our trust in God grows. Because Tina and Bob are prayerful people, they were able to trust in God during this "needy" time in their lives.

Authentic prayer leads us to greater trust in God; it lessens our anxieties and worries. Prayer becomes a life-changing experience the more we trust in God and less in ourselves. As someone once said: "Prayer does not change things, it changes people." The beautiful image of the potter's vessel portrays this truth: "Then the word of the Lord came to me. Can I not do to you, house of Israel, as this potter has done? says the Lord. Indeed, like clay in the hand of the potter, so are you in my hand, house of Israel" (Jeremiah 18:5–6). Through prayer the deeper fears and anxieties of our hearts can be transformed into attitudes of trust and love. Our hearts undergo a *metanoia*, a transformation, and the things and events of our lives take on new meaning. We become clay in God's hands.

The letter to the Hebrews says: "Keep your eyes fixed on Jesus, who inspires and perfects your faith" (12:2). By keeping our eyes on God, by listening in prayer, we grow more deeply aware of God's unconditional love—that God cares for us more than the birds of the air and the lilies of the field. Through prayer we become aware of the deepest mystery of life—that God is all in all, that God is a rock and refuge, that God's kingdom of holiness is within us and within each person we meet.

CONCLUSION

The familiar story of the lilies of the field presents to us a vital challenge—a challenge which we encounter daily. This challenge is wrapped in the blanket of a decision: a choice to live life to its fullness as a mystery, or to live life in its smallness as a problem. If we choose to view and live life as a problem, the kingdom of God cannot live deeply within us; God's way of holiness grows dim. If we choose to perceive and live life as a mystery, then the kingdom of God will be vibrant and alive within and around us. We will be a strength for others, a light burning bright in so much darkness in the world.

Being with God

PONDERING

Reflect on the way that you view life. Do you see it as a mystery to be lived? Or is it a series of problems to be solved? What do you need in your life to make your life more meaningful? What is the "why" that you live for?

What are the priorities in your life? Ponder each of these carefully. Look at them through God's eyes. What are God's priorities for you? Are they the same as your priorities? Or are they different from yours?

What is your prayer life like? Does it change you—your attitudes, feelings, and behaviors?

SHARING

God of my life, you desire that I see my life as you see it—an unfolding gift each day. You want to be the center of my life, but so often other realities are at the center. Help me to see what blocks me from living my life to the fullest. Give me the grace to put you first in my life and all my decisions.

God of my journey, walk with me through the ups and downs of life. When I am anxious, give me your peace. When I am sad, give me your joy. When I get lost, come and find me and show me the way. When I am alone, come and be my closest friend.

God of my searching, give me the grace to seek you and your way of holiness first. Let my searching heart find a resting place in you. Let my craving heart be soothed with your gentle love. Let my fearful heart find an oasis of safety in you. Give me trust to know my life is in your hands.

LISTENING

My searching one, know that my love surrounds you as a warm blanket. I hold you secure in my heart. Put your trust in me. Be attentive to my heart so I can reveal to you the meaning of your life. Your life has the deepest meaning in me. Your thirst, your longing, your craving can only be satisfied in me. Come and drink from the well of salvation, for I am the Living Water that will quench your thirst.

RESPONDING

Our bodies represent what is in our spirits. Through body movement we can get more deeply in touch with our outlook on life. Use gestures to show what you are like when you see life as an unfolding mystery, and what you are like when your life becomes a series of problems. What feelings are evoked in you with each set of gestures? Journal about this body movement experience.

See each reality of your life—your home, food, clothing, people—as God providing for you. Take time to savor and enjoy the food you eat and drink today. Take time to smell the flowers, and to enjoy the people who are part of your life.

God Showing Us the Way

How Do I Get There?

I beg you through the mercy of God to offer your bodies as a living sacrifice holy and acceptable to God, your spiritual worship. Do not conform yourselves to this age but be transformed by the renewal of your mind, so that you may discern what is God's will, what is good, pleasing and perfect.

Just as each of us has one body with many members, and not all the members have the same function, so too we, though many, are one body in Christ and individually members one of another. We have gifts that differ according to the favor bestowed on all of us....

Your love must be sincere. Detest what is evil, cling to what is good. Love one another with the affection of brothers and sisters. Anticipate each other in showing respect...(Romans 12:1-2, 4-5, 9-10).

How many times in our lives have we asked the very practical question: How do I get there? When we were children our mother may have sent us to the store, and we asked: "Mom, how do I get there?" When we first received our driver's license and were so excited about driving, we would drive anywhere our parents asked us to. Maybe our father would ask us to go pick up our little brother or sister at a friend's house, and we would say: "Sure, dad, how do I get there?" As adults possibly our job requires us to go on a business trip many miles away, so we take out a map to find out: How do I get there?

In Romans 12 Paul explains how we can get where we are going on our spiritual journey as we strive to love God and one another. Paul gives us a roadmap with clear signs along the way to our destination. First, he states the *goal* of the Christian life—where are we going? Second, Paul comments on the use of the *gifts* in the Christian community—how do we reach this goal? Lastly, he gives the nitty-gritty *guidelines* necessary to reach our goal—how are we going to reach our destination in the practical day-to-day situations of our lives? Through examining these three dimensions of our life—its goal, gifts, and guidelines, we see a clear roadmap of highways and roads which will lead us to our destination—total union with God.

OUR GOAL:
SURRENDERING OURSELVES TO GOD

At the beginning of this reading the goal of our lives is stated clearly and succinctly—to offer ourselves wholly and entirely to God as "a living sacrifice." This is not only a spiritual offering, an offering of our minds and spirits. It is a total giving of ourselves—our minds, spirits, hearts, *and* our bodies. Paul says, "Offer your *bodies* as a living sacrifice holy and acceptable to God, your spiritual worship." True worship of God is not only coming together on Sundays to praise the Lord, but more importantly it is the offering of our daily lives to God in love and surrender—work, fun, aggravations, and joys. It means putting on the mind of Christ, a *new mind*, so that our "behavior will change and we will be transformed." Through the daily offering of ourselves to God and the transformation of our minds and hearts, we will be able "to discover the will of God and know what is good and pleasing and perfect to God."

What a beautiful, yet challenging goal we have as followers of Christ! To give ourselves completely to God, holding nothing back, as Jesus gave himself completely to the Father. What a profound realization to know that God wants, not earthly sacrifices and things, but us—our entire selves. God loves each of us so much that God wants us continually to offer back the true spiritual worship of our lives and ourselves—spirit, mind, heart, and body.

OUR GIFTS: GOD GIVING TO US

The beautiful reality about our spiritual journey is that even though we all have the same destination, the same goal, we do not have to arrive there in exactly the same way. How do I get there? Our God gives us different highways to reach the same place, a variety of gifts to achieve the same goal.

In the second part of Romans 12 Paul stresses that even though we are one body, we do not have the same functions. Just as each of our bodies has many parts and each part has a separate function, so all of us, although one body in Christ, have different *gifts*. Our gifts differ according to the grace given to us. How boring life would be if we all took the same highway, the same paths, and had the same gifts. What a blessing unity and diversity is— that we all strive toward the same goal, we all desire union with God, yet we have diverse gifts and talents. Each person has a task to do. When we use our gifts and perform our tasks, the Christian community functions in a vibrant and life-giving way.

This passage enumerates seven gifts or tasks which are needed to build up the body of Christ. There is the gift of prophecy—prophets are those who proclaim the word of God with conviction because they have experienced the power of the word themselves. The gift of ministry, that is, the gift of practical service, is doing good deeds for others. There is the gift of teaching—explaining to others the word of God which has been proclaimed. The gift of exhortation—giving others encouragement. There is the gift of giving alms—sharing generously with others our material goods. The gift of leadership—serving others in community in an official capacity. Finally, there is the gift of showing mercy—treating others with kindness and concern, and being willing to forgive another unconditionally, without limits.

These seven gifts are only a few of the many, many gifts that make up the body of Christ. Each of us has special gifts that we bring to the community. We need to reflect on these questions: What gifts do I offer to my family? to the people that I associate with each day? to the people I work with? to society? to the church? Remember! God has given us some tasks to perform while we are here on earth. What we leave undone will never be done by anyone else, because we bring our own unique personality and talents to our tasks.

We need to keep in mind always the words which Jesus said to his disciples: "What you have received as a gift, give as a gift" (Matthew 10:8). By sharing our gifts with others, we are reaching our ultimate goal of offering ourselves in true spiritual worship to God. "What you are is God's gift to you; what you make of yourself, what you give of yourself, is your gift to God."

GUIDELINES: HOW WE LIVE IN GOD

In Romans 12 after Paul says where we are going—our goal, and how we get there—through the use of our gifts, he gives us some specific directions to help us reach our goal and states some practical principles to help us use our gifts in the nitty-gritty circumstances of our lives. Paul enumerates concrete *guidelines* for our daily living. He goes to the heart of Christian relationships. He gives us the smaller roads to reach our destination—the roads which turn off from the highways and which will enable us to reach our goal.

First, Paul gives us ten directives for everyday life. "Your love must be sincere"—there must be no hypocrisy, no play-acting, no ulterior motives. "Detest what is evil and cling to what is good"—we must not only avoid evil, but more positively, go after goodness. "Love one another with the affection of brothers and sisters"—we must love each other because we are members of one family, the family of God. "Have a profound respect for each other"—love without respect for others' rights and uniqueness is not love at all. "Do not grow slack"—there is no room for lethargy, only intensity. "The Christian may burn out, but he must not rust out," says William Barclay. "Be fervent in spirit"—Jesus himself says we are to be hot or cold, that he will "vomit you out of my mouth" if we are lukewarm.

"The One whom you serve is the Lord"—a reminder to us that our love for one another is an essential way of loving God. "Rejoice in hope, be patient under trial"—the test of our love for God and others is our faithfulness even when we are suffering and all seems hopeless. "Persevere in prayer"—it is prayer that will give us the strength to continue to be faithful. "If any of the saints are in need you must share with them; and you should make hospitality your special care"—in a self-seeking society intent on getting, the Christian is focused on giving. "Christianity is the religion of the open hand, the open heart, and the open door."

After Paul gives us these ten directives, these ten roadways, for ordinary everyday life, he takes us along pathways which we might not naturally follow. He gives us principles about how we are to treat those we do not like, those who hurt us, those who are our enemies. Our natural reaction may be to avoid or take revenge on such people, but Paul gives us some positive directives. "Bless those who persecute you; bless and do not curse them." We have two beautiful examples of this in the New Testament. Jesus himself cries out on the cross: "Father, forgive them for they do not know what they are doing." Stephen, following the example of his Lord and master, cries out almost the same words while he is being stoned to death. We must also follow Jesus' example.

"...Have the same attitude toward all. Put away ambitious thoughts and associate with those who are lowly." No matter whether we like someone or not, we must have the same attitude of love and respect for that person as for someone we like. We must be willing to associate with all kinds of people.

"...Never repay injury with injury...never try to get revenge...do not be conquered by evil but conquer evil with good." We must treat people who hurt us with kindness rather than vengeance: "Vengeance may break a per-

son's spirit; but kindness will break that person's heart,"
says Barclay. To give in to vengeance is to allow ourselves to
be conquered by evil. Evil can never be conquered by evil:
"The only way to destroy an enemy is to make that person
a friend."

CONCLUSION

Romans 12 gives us a complete and thorough map for
our spiritual journey. Indeed it is a roadmap that describes
our destination and the way to get there. Our *goal,* our destination, as followers of Jesus Christ is to offer ourselves
completely to God in true spiritual worship. The *gifts* that
God has given us are the highways along which we travel
to reach our destination. The *guidelines,* the side roads
which we take along the way, are the principles and nitty-
gritty pathways along which we must travel in order to
offer ourselves completely to God. How do I get there?
How do I reach the ultimate fulfillment of my life in God?
By meditating frequently on this practical and powerful
passage in Romans, we will understand better the highways, the paths, we must follow.

Being with God

PONDERING

Ponder the goal of your life as a follower of Jesus—to
offer yourself completely to God. How complete is your
surrender to God now in your life? What are you holding
back from God?

Consider how you use your gifts for the kingdom.
What are the gifts that God has given you for the service

of others? Which gifts are you using now and which ones are lying dormant? How do you feel about the unique gifts God has given you?

Reflect on your relationships with others, especially those who are a part of your daily life—your family, community, coworkers, friends. How are you living the directives and principles enumerated above? What are your attitudes toward the various people in your everyday life? Ask God for the qualities of Christian love that are missing in your relationships.

SHARING

My God and my all, give me the grace to offer myself to you in complete surrender. Help me to see those areas in myself that I am holding back, and to surrender them. Thank you for your desire for total union with me.

Giving God, thank you for the many gifts you have given to me. Help me to use them generously to help others grow closer to you. Help me to see those gifts that still lie dormant within me. Let me give with a generous heart, not counting the cost. Let me give with a free heart, not expecting anything in return.

God of unbounded love, help me to see others as you see them and to love others with your heart. Let my love for others be utterly sincere. Give me a forbearing and forgiving heart, a heart that accepts all people as they are.

LISTENING

My beloved, put your life in my hands and I will give you my life. Know that it is in giving all to me that you will receive all. You will receive my mind to understand with, my eyes to see

*with, my heart to love with. Just surrender your whole self to me
and you will be blessed with abundant gifts of love and service.*

*Put your trust in me. I will lead you along the right paths.
In surrendering to me you will never be lost. I will always show
you the way–the way to a fuller life in the Spirit. Keep your eyes
fixed on me and I will show you the way to true joy, deep peace,
and everlasting love.*

RESPONDING

Draw the roadmap of your spiritual journey as out-
lined in Romans 12 with the Goal, Gifts, and Guidelines.
Be creative in your drawing.

In your journal list all the gifts God has given to you
and describe how you use them or do not use them. Share
your reflections with a friend or two and ask them what
gifts they see in you that you have not mentioned.

Contemplate a person in your life right now whom
you are struggling to love. Write down the negative feelings and attitudes you have toward this person, and the
positive ones you would like to have. Ask God for the grace
to love this person with these positive feelings and attitudes, to see this person as God sees him or her.

Conclusion

Praying With Scripture

Scripture speaks personally to us about our journey with God. Through our being with scripture in a relational and contemplative way, we discover verses and stories that speak to our relationship with God. Through praying with scripture we come to know God in a heartfelt way. The words in the Bible become the word of God experienced deep in our hearts. Through contemplating scripture our hearts become like soft soil that receives seeds of truth about God and ourselves, and absorbs the rain of Living Waters. Soon our lives become a beautiful garden of the life of God.

To continue your contemplation of scripture, I suggest scripture quotes for you to ponder, listen to, and respond to. To foster the habit of sharing with God feelings from your heart, I include scripture passages with the "sharing" expression of prayer. I invite you to use these or any other scriptures that speak to your heart in various moments of your journey of love.

SCRIPTURAL QUOTES TO PONDER

"Truly you have formed my inmost being;
  you knit me in my mother's womb.
I give you thanks that I am fearfully, wonderfully made;
  wonderful are your works" (Psalm 139:13–14).

"Stronger than death is love" (Songs 8:6).

"When I called, you answered me;
  you built up strength within me" (Psalm 138:3).

"The Lord is my light and my salvation;
  whom should I fear?
The Lord is my life's refuge;
  of whom should I be afraid?" (Psalm 27:1).

"I will never desert you, nor will I forsake you."

"The Lord sees not appearances, but what is in the heart."

"You duped me, O Lord, and I let myself be duped:
    you were too strong for me, and you triumphed"
    (Jeremiah 20:7).

"By waiting and by calm you shall be saved,
    in quiet and in trust your strength lies" (Isaiah 30:15).

"Naked I came forth from my mother's womb,
    and naked shall I go back again.
The Lord gave and the Lord has taken away;
    blessed be the name of the Lord!" (Job 1:21).

"I have been grasped by Christ" (Philippians 3:12).

"For human beings it is impossible,
    but for God all things are possible" (Matthew 19:26).

"In God who is the source of my strength
    I have strength for everything" (Philippians 4:13).

"To me 'life' means Christ" (Philippians 1:21).

"The life I live now is not my own;
Christ is living in me" (Galatians 2:20).

"I am certain that neither death nor life,
neither the present nor the future,
neither height nor depth nor any other creature,
will be able to separate us from the love of God
that comes to us in Christ Jesus" (Romans 8:38–39).

"Come by yourselves to an out of the way place
and rest awhile" (Mark 6:31).

SCRIPTURAL QUOTES WITH PRAYERS

"Be still and know that I am God."
Thank you, God, for letting me rest in your stillness and quietness. Thank you for simply allowing me to be with you. You are everything to me; you are my all. In you my deepest needs and desires will be fulfilled. Continue to make me one with you, my God, no matter how much and how deeply I need to be stripped. Give me only your love and your grace—with these I am rich enough and desire nothing more.

"Stir into flame the gift that God has given you" (1 Timothy 1:6).
I am so blessed, my God! You have given me many gifts and allowed me to develop them over the years. I feel

overwhelmed by the many ways you have blessed and gifted me. You have called me to be your special possession.
You love me tenderly, graciously, and deeply. Thank you
for calling me to bring your love to others. Give me your
heart with which to love others. Thank you for giving me a
burning desire to serve you. Give me the courage to live
and speak your word. May I always give you the praise and
glory you deserve.

*"Jesus asks the blind man, 'What do you want from me?'" (Mark
11:51).*
 I need a lot from you today, Jesus. I ask you to free me
from my resentments, inner hangups, insecurities, feelings
of inferiority, fear. Help me to see people and the world as
you see them. Give me wisdom, knowledge, and discern-
ment. Give me your heart, Jesus, to love with, because my
heart is feeble today.

*"More tortuous than all else is the human heart, beyond remedy;
who can understand it?" (Jeremiah 17:9).*
 Lord, my God, I give you praise and honor this day. I
give you this poor heart of mine, which is tortured by its
own needs and desires. Dear God, give me the grace to
put all of my trust in you, to expect nothing from any
human being. Give me the gift and grace of unconditional
love. Give me the grace to find my strength in you and
your love. You seem to be stripping me to the core of my
being. I do not know why and at times I don't know if I
can bear it. Help me to unite the pain of my heart to yours,
to take up my cross and follow you, to lose my life so that I
can find life and true freedom.

"Fear is useless; what is needed is trust" (Mark 5:36).
 God of my heart, you see the fears in my heart and

how often I lack faith and trust. Your power is beyond all comprehension, and you do so many things for my greater good. Give me the grace to always put Jesus at the center of my life, no matter what the cost. May I never put my trust in another person but only in you, because in you I find salvation, healing, and forgiveness of my sins. I beg of you to increase within me your gifts of trust and faith. Thank you for showing me your way and for helping me to be strong when I am weak.

"He vanished from their sight" (Luke 24:31).

Dear God, you seem so distant today. You seem to have vanished from my sight. I have felt you so close to me and now you seem to have disappeared. Help me to know and believe that you are with me at all times, even when you hide your face from me. Help me to be faithful to you in your absence. Give me the insight to see if there is something in me that is preventing me from seeing you.

"All I want is to know Christ and to share in his resurrection by reproducing the pattern of his death....I count all else as loss if only I can have Christ" (Philippians 3:10, 8).

God, my creator, this is my prayer from the depths of my heart. I want Christ to be everything. I am convinced now more than ever that this is the only way it can be—that Jesus must be my life and that my one desire is to know him and experience his death and resurrection. Forgive me my failures and sins; strengthen me through your life and love. Give me the grace to forfeit everything in order to have Christ—this has been both my struggle and my desire. With your help, I can surrender all to you.

"Abide in me as I abide in you" (John 15:4).

This is my desire, Jesus, to abide in you, to live in you.

Continue to draw me, Lord. Help me to be more completely one with you. I want every fiber of my being—my thoughts, feelings, heart, mind, spirit, body—to abide in you. Prune me of those attitudes and patterns of behavior that cause my abiding in you and your abiding in me to be incomplete. I love you, Jesus, and want always that you be the root and foundation of my life.